Countries Around the World

Estonia

Richard Spilsbury

Heinemann Library
Chicago, Illinois

www.heinemannraintree.com

Visit our website to find out more information about Heinemann-Raintree books.

To order:

☎ Phone 888-454-2279

⌨ Visit www.heinemannraintree.com to browse our catalog and order online.

Edited by Kate de Villiers and Vaarunika Dharmapala
Designed by Joanna Hinton-Malivoire
Original illustrations © Capstone Global Library Ltd 2011
Illustrated by Oxford Designers & Illustrators
Picture research by Ruth Blair
Originated by Capstone Global Library Ltd
Printed and bound in China by CTPS

15 14 13 12 11
10 9 8 7 6 5 4 3 2 1

Library of Congress Cataloging-in-Publication Data
Spilsbury, Richard.
 Estonia / Richard and Louise Spilsbury.
  p. cm.—(Countries around the world)
 Includes bibliographical references and index.
 ISBN 978-1-4329-5202-0 (hc)—ISBN 978-1-4329-5227-3 (pb) 1. Estonia—Juvenile literature. I.Spilsbury, Louise. II. Title.
 DK503.23.S66 2012
 947.98—dc22   2010039274

Acknowledgments
We would like to thank the following for permission to reproduce photographs: Alamy p. 7 (© World History Archive), p. 17 (© Steve Vanstone), p. 18 (© Sven Zacek), p. 27 (© Hemis), pp. 28, 29, 31 (© Jaak Nilson), p. 30 (© TVeermae_Tallinn_Estonia), p. 33 (© isifa Image Service s.r.o.), p. 35 (© Jon Hicks); Corbis p. 8 (© Bettmann), p. 9, **pp. 11**, 22 (© INTS KALNINS/X02120/Reuters), p. 32 (© Kai Pfaffenbach/Reuters); Photolibrary p. 19 (© Sven Zacek/OSF), p. 20 (ANDRE MASLENNIKOV/Still Pictures), p. 21 (Sven Zacek/OSF), p. 25 (Mattes/Mauritius); Shutterstock p. 5 (© Galchenkova Ludmila), p. 13 (© yui), p. 15 (© zahradales), p. 26 (© StockLite), p. 34 (© MikeEst), p. 37 (© Aleksi Markku), p. 46 (© pdesign).

Cover photograph of Mundi Street, Tallinn, reproduced with permission of Alamy (© TVeermae_Tallinn_Estonia).

We would like to thank Daniel Block for his invaluable help in the preparation of this book.

Every effort has been made to contact copyright holders of material reproduced in this book. Any omissions will be rectified in subsequent printings if notice is given to the publisher.

Disclaimer
All the Internet addresses (URLs) given in this book were valid at the time of going to press. However, due to the dynamic nature of the Internet, some addresses may have changed, or sites may have changed or ceased to exist since publication. While the author and publisher regret any inconvenience this may cause readers, no responsibility for any such changes can be accepted by either the author or the publisher.

Contents

Some words in the book are in bold, **like this**. You can find out what they mean by looking in the glossary.

Introducing Estonia

What do you know about Estonia? That it is a cold, dark place near the North Pole? Estonia is actually part of northern Europe. It is bordered by Latvia, Russia, the Baltic Sea, and the Gulf of Finland. The coast of Estonia has 1,500 islands and many white, sandy beaches. Inland there are dense forests, **bogs**, and lakes, which are home to a wide range of wildlife.

Estonia today is a modern, independent nation. It has rich **natural resources** and strong trading links with nearby Finland and other countries bordering the Baltic Sea. The small Estonian population is generally well-educated, healthy, and fairly wealthy. However, Estonia was very different in the past.

Foreign rulers

For centuries, Estonia was ruled by other countries that wanted control of its position in Europe. These countries included Sweden, Germany, and Russia. In those days, Estonians were known simply as "country folk" by their rulers. The country gained its independence in the first half of the twentieth century, only to lose it again not long afterward. It wasn't until 1991 that it finally regained independence once more.

The history of Estonia may explain why its people have a strong cultural identity. Hundreds of thousands of Estonians crowd together every few years to hear vast choirs of singers perform national folk songs.

How to say...

Hello! *Tere!* (Tehray!)
Welcome *Tere tulemast* (Tehray tooluhmast)
Pleased to meet you. *Meeldiv teid kohata.* (Maildiv tade cohottah.)
I'm sorry, I don't speak Estonian. *Vabandage, ma ei räägi eesti keelt.* (Vabandoggeh ma-ee raggy esty kelt.)
Goodbye *Head aega* (Heyadd eye-eager)

This is the beautiful old city center of Tallinn, the capital of Estonia.

History: Invasion and Independence

The land now known as Estonia was first inhabited about 13,000 years ago. Around 100 BCE, the people who lived there were known as *Aestii*, which means the "eastern people." The country grew into an important trading center, and attracted Vikings and other pirate invaders during the next half century. During the **medieval** period, Germans known as the Teutonic Knights invaded the country and brought the **Christian** religion with them.

From the 1200s to the 1500s, German landowners built castles on rich estates across Estonia, from which they made their fortunes. In the 1600s, Sweden was victorious in wars against Russia and ruled Estonia for 80 years. During this time, the whole country was united under one ruler, peasants were given more freedom, and the Estonian **economy** grew.

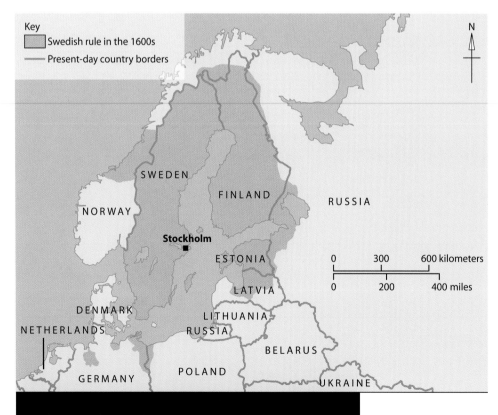

This map shows when Estonia was ruled by Sweden.

Russian rule

After a period of **plague**, **famine**, and unrest, the country was conquered by Russia in the Great Northern War (1700–1721). Russia ruled Estonia from St. Petersburg, its capital. German landowners retained local control over the peasants making up most of Estonia's population. Peasants had to work on the landowners' land and hand over most of what they farmed. They did not have the right to own land or even to have last names until the early 1800s!

In 1558, Ivan the Terrible, the ruler of Russia, sent his army into Estonia. He wanted to use it as a base from which to trade with the rest of Europe.

These Estonian refugees traveled to the United States in 1946 to escape the Soviet invasion.

First freedom

In the late 1800s, many Estonians wanted to take back their country. People rediscovered Estonian traditions, and Estonian-language newspapers were published. In 1918, Estonia declared its independence. At the same time, there was a **revolution** in Russia. Estonia and its **allies** fought the War of Independence from 1918 to 1920 and managed to defeat the Russian forces. The country became independent, and its economy grew.

However, in 1940 the **Soviet Union occupied** Estonia. Many Estonians were sent to work and died in **labor camps**. Then, in 1941, the Germans invaded. Some Estonians welcomed Germany's invasion, but **Nazi** forces proved to be just as brutal as the Soviets. In 1944, the Soviet Union retook Estonia. In total, around a quarter of the Estonian population died in World War II, and more fled the country or went into hiding in the forests to escape **persecution**.

Estonia after the war

Estonians feared they would lose their national identity under the influence of Soviet settlers and rulers. When the Soviet economy started to fail in the 1980s, several regions, including the Baltic states of Estonia, Latvia, and Lithuania, pushed for independence. Protest rallies took place, and hundreds of thousands of people sang Estonian national songs. This was called the Singing Revolution. By 1991, Estonia was independent again, and the Soviet Union had collapsed.

AUGUST SABBE (1909–1978)

August Sabbe was one of 14,000 Estonian rebels known as the Forest Brothers. From 1944 to 1953, these rebels lived in forest camps, hiding from and attacking Soviet troops. After the Brothers separated, Sabbe stayed in hiding for the rest of his life.

During the Singing Revolution, more than two million people across the Baltic region, including Estonia, joined hands and sang songs in protest against Soviet rule.

Modern Estonia

After independence, Estonia formed a stable government. It introduced the *kroon* as its **currency**, and built economic and political ties with Western Europe rather than Russia. The country became a member of the North Atlantic Treaty Organization (**NATO**) and the European Union (**EU**) in 2004. Estonians celebrate those who fought for independence with festivals, songs, and monuments. The country's flag is also a reminder of this.

The Estonian population is small at 1.3 million—that's only about 30 people for every square kilometer of the country. Most people are between 15 and 64 years of age and live in cities or towns. Two-thirds of the population is of the Estonian **ethnic group**. Most of the rest are Russians whose **ancestors** were invaders or settlers in the past. Many of these people still speak Russian as their first language.

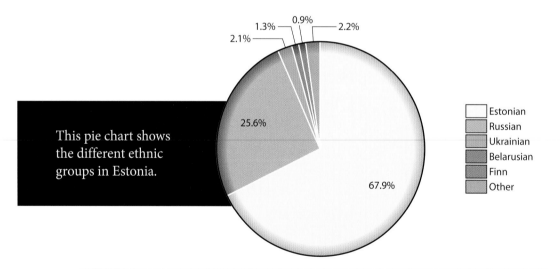

This pie chart shows the different ethnic groups in Estonia.

- Estonian
- Russian
- Ukrainian
- Belarusian
- Finn
- Other

YOUNG PEOPLE

St. John's Day (*Jaanipäev*) takes place on June 24—the day after Victory Day in the War for Independence. It is an important national festival for the whole family in Estonia. Young people take part in singing national songs, traditional dancing, and even jumping over bonfires using long poles!

A child waves the Estonian flag during a celebration in the capital city, Tallinn.

Daily life

Popular names in Estonia include:

Boys' names: Markus, Rasmus, Martin, Aleksandr

Girls' names: Anastasia, Laura, Maria, Sandra

Last names: Many last names are also types of trees common in Estonia! They include Saar (ash), Tamm (oak), Lepik (alder), and Kask (birch).

Regions and Resources: Trees, Water, and the Economy

Estonia is a very flat country and is half covered with pine, spruce, or birch forest. Nearly a quarter of the country's area is wetland and **bogs**. Many bogs are on layers of **peat** soil of up to 55 feet (17 meters) thick! The bogs are home to some unusual plants, including the sundew, which traps flies to eat. The rest of Estonia is grassy meadow, farmland, and settlements. Estonia has thousands of lakes and rivers, including giant Lake Peipus in the east. Its long coastline bordering the cold Baltic Sea has rocky cliffs and many white, sandy beaches.

Climate

The climate (normal pattern of weather) of Estonia is influenced by the Baltic Sea. Moist air from over the sea blows into the land. This makes summers and autumns drizzly or **humid**. In winter, the moist air freezes into thick snow. The temperature can reach 86°F (30°C) in summer but always drops well below 32°F (0°C) in winter because cold air blows in from Russia.

This map shows the land heights above sea level of Estonia and its neighbors.

Daily life

It never gets totally dark during the Estonian summer, between May and July. This is because Estonia is never completely shaded from the Sun's light. People have late night picnics, swim in lakes, visit the zoo, or have parties to celebrate the "white nights."

In winter, water can freeze over so thickly that cars can drive across it.

The regions of Estonia

Estonia is divided up into five regions and each has different characteristics:

Pohja-Eesti

The northern region of Pohja-Eesti includes Estonia's capital city, Tallinn. Tallinn's **medieval** center dates back to the 1100s and is surrounded by many modern buildings. This region has the densest population and a lot of coastline.

Kesk-Eesti

The rich soil of Kesk-Eesti, south of Pohja-Eesti, has made it the center for farming in Estonia.

Kirde-Eesti

The eastern region of Kirde-Eesti includes industrial cities, such as Narva.

Lõuna-Eesti

The southern region of Lõuna-Eesti is naturally beautiful with many lakes, bogs, and rolling hills. Its major city, Tartu, is one of the cultural and educational centers of the country.

Lääne-Eesti

The beaches, sheltered waters, and islands of the western region of Lääne-Eesti attract many tourists. Saaremaaa, the largest island in Estonia, is famous for its windmills. The island of Kihnu was traditionally run by women while the men went to sea to fish.

How to say...

beach *mererand* (mayrerand) **lake** *järv* (yairve)
bog *soo* (sue) **mountain** *magi* (margee)
island *saar* (saah) **river** *jõgi* (yergee)

Daily life

When winter ice and snow melts from the land surface in spring, Estonian rivers overflow and cause flooding, especially in Lõuna-Eesti. Estonians call this wet period the "fifth season." Today, in order to cope, people build their homes on stilts to raise them above the water level. But in the past, everyone—including farm animals—simply moved upstairs when the house flooded!

The island of Hiiumaa in Lääne-Eesti has a small population and many beautiful, isolated beaches.

Resources

Estonia has many resources people use and need. Over two-thirds of Estonian forest is managed for the timber industry. Trees are cut down for timber or to make wood products. Then the land is replanted with new trees. There is an abundance of fresh water for Estonian people and industries to use. The rich peat from Estonian bogs is used for growing plants, and for fuel. Estonia has large quantities of **minerals**, including oil shale. Oil shale is a special rock containing sticky oil used as fuel in most Estonian power stations.

Economy

The GDP (gross domestic product) is the total value of services and goods produced by a country each year. In Estonia, the GDP is equivalent to $18,700 for each citizen. This is far less than in the United States, but more than in Russia.

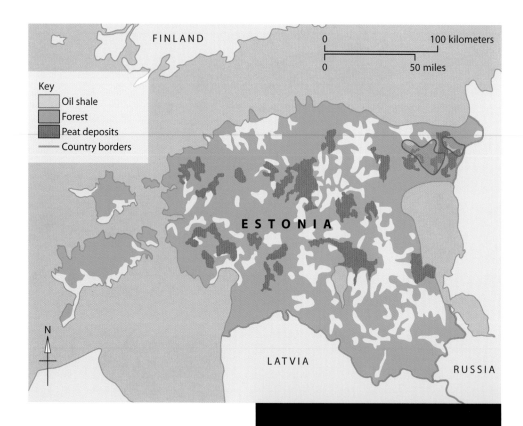

This map shows where Estonia's main resources are found.

Most Estonians work in **service industries**, which include jobs in hotels, restaurants, shops, and schools. The international telecommunications company Skype began in Estonia and employs hundreds of people in Tallinn. Some Estonians are farmers and fishermen. The country trades mostly with other countries nearby, including Finland, Sweden, and Russia. It **imports** products such as fuel for vehicles, and its **exports** include timber and machinery.

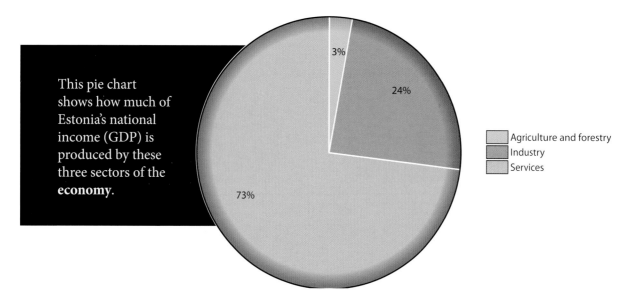

This pie chart shows how much of Estonia's national income (GDP) is produced by these three sectors of the **economy**.

3%

24%

73%

- Agriculture and forestry
- Industry
- Services

Around 10 percent of Estonians work in the country's timber industry.

Wildlife: Habitats and Threats

The dense trees and sheltered spaces of Estonian forests are home to many species of animals. These include brown bears, wolves, elk, wild boar, and beavers. Many flies, dragonflies, **amphibians**, and fish, such as pike, live in the wetlands. In some places, pond bats flap over lakes catching small flies to eat. Summer visitors to Estonia need to wear insect repellent to ward off the billions of mosquitoes that breed in the **bogs**. Hundreds of thousands of ducks, geese, and swans travel over Estonia in spring, stopping to feed in coastal wetlands.

Habitat destruction

Wildlife populations fall when their **habitat** is disturbed by human activity. In Estonia, large areas of forest and meadow in the northeast have been dug up to mine oil shale (see page 16). Cutting down forests also destroys wildlife habitats. For example, flying squirrels find places to breed and shelter in large trees in old, natural forests, but not in new **plantations**.

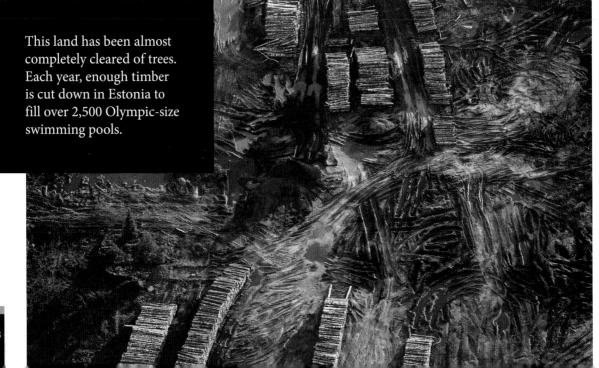

This land has been almost completely cleared of trees. Each year, enough timber is cut down in Estonia to fill over 2,500 Olympic-size swimming pools.

Elk are the largest land animals in Estonia, with adults reaching around 6 feet (1.8 meters) at shoulder height.

How to say...

bear *karu* (karoo)
elk *põder* (poe-der)
mosquito *moskiito* (moskeetoh)
owl *öökull* (erkool)
pike *haug* (howg)
wolf *hunt* (hoont)

Many of Estonia's bogs have been drained to make digging **peat** easier. Draining destroys habitats and contributes to **global warming**. Carbon dioxide and methane gas escape from the ground and trap heat in Earth's atmosphere. European gardening companies want the Estonian government to let them buy more of the country's peat, putting even more pressure on Estonia's natural habitats.

Pollution

A lot of soil **pollution** was caused by the Russian army when it left Estonia in the 1990s. They dumped thousands of tons of fuel on the land rather than transport it back to Russia. Fewer plants can grow on polluted land. Lake and wetland animals are affected when polluted soil, mine waste, and farm chemicals wash off the land. For example, frogs cannot breathe through their skins in polluted water.

Chemicals and oil spilled from ships and coastal factories in Estonia and Russia have made the Baltic Sea one of the most polluted in the world. Numbers of fish, such as herring, are falling as a result, and this is affecting the fishing industry.

Mining produces a lot of waste. When this waste gets washed into rivers, it causes pollution.

Protecting habitats and wildlife

Estonia protects one-tenth of its land as nature and landscape reserves. This means that the land and the wildlife that live on it are cared for. In southern Estonia, wardens monitor and protect a nest of rare lesser-spotted eagles.

There are five national parks in the country, of which the largest is the old forest at Lahemaa, near Tallinn. Soomaa National Park is the best-known bog area in the country. The entrance fees paid by its many visitors are used to help conserve the habitat.

The population of Eurasian cranes in Estonia is growing, due to the protection of their breeding grounds in the country's wetlands.

YOUNG PEOPLE

Every May since 1980, young Estonians at school and college have been taking part in National **Conservation** Month in the country. The idea was originally to make Estonians living in cities more aware of the countryside and its conservation issues. Today, thousands of youngsters study wildlife, take nature walks, and help with conservation projects.

Infrastructure: State, Education, and Health

Estonian people elect their government every four years. Anyone age 18 and over can vote for members of different political parties. The Estonian parliament (*Riigikogu*) is made up of 101 seats, and the number of seats each party has depends on the results of the election.

The *Riigikogu* elects a president as **head of state** (public representative) of the country. The president from 2006–2011 was Toomas-Hendrik Ilves. The president appoints a prime minister from the *Riigikogu* to lead the government. The government makes laws, decides how Estonia spends its money, and appoints leaders in the army and other organizations.

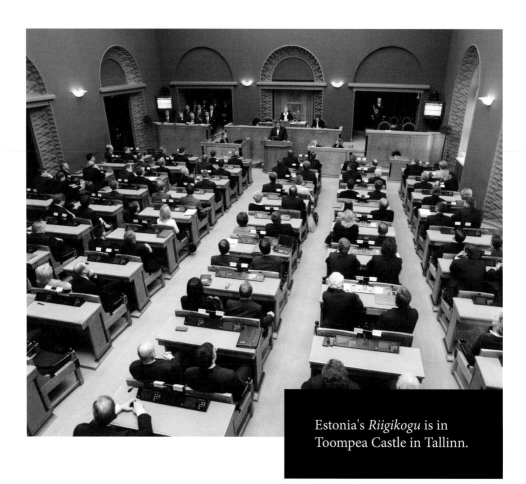

Estonia's *Riigikogu* is in Toompea Castle in Tallinn.

Money

In 2011, the **euro** replaced the *kroon* as Estonian **currency**. Estonia made the change in order to increase trade with countries that already use the euro, such as Finland. Trade increases because companies do not have to pay banks to change currency into euros when people buy things. Prices in Estonia are similar to those in other parts of Europe. One euro buys about one liter (0.26 gallon) of gasoline, a dozen eggs, or a large loaf of bread.

This map shows the main transportation networks in Estonia.

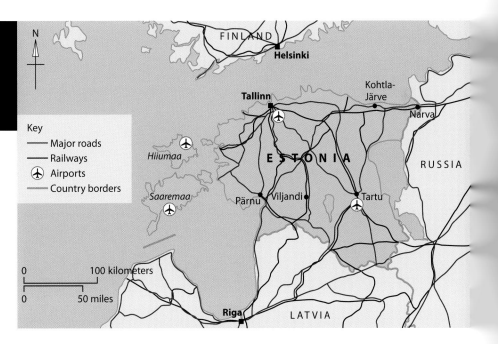

LENNART MERI (1929-2006)

When the **Soviet Union** seized Estonia in 1940, Lennert Meri's family was sent to a **labor camp**. As a boy, he worked as a potato peeler. He became a writer after returning to Estonia. Meri campaigned against the problems of Soviet **occupation**, such as the way industry was spoiling the countryside. Meri established contact between Estonia and Western countries, which recognized the country's independence. He became the first president of Estonia in 1992, and remained in the postition until 2001.

Education

Estonian children have to go to school between the ages of 7 and 16. The government provides free education, although some parents send their children to private schools. Pupils never wear school uniforms at state schools. Over two-thirds of children study in Estonian, but most of the rest study partly in Russian because they normally speak Russian at home.

The school year starts on September 1, when students traditionally give flowers to their new teachers. Primary students study reading and writing, math, science or geography, art, music, and PE. The school day is from 8:00 a.m. until 3:00 p.m., and periods usually last 45 minutes. At the end of each year, pupils are tested in math, literacy, and a subject of their choice.

At the age of 16 students may go to high schools, called gymnasiums, to study a wide range of academic subjects, usually including English and another language. They can also attend institutes to learn jobs, such as in tourism or engineering.

After high school, 46 percent of students go to one of ten Estonian universities, or to some other form of higher education. Over a third of Estonians have a university degree, which is a higher proportion than in most European countries.

YOUNG PEOPLE

In Estonia, there are over 200 hobby schools for young people. They can attend these after school, on weekends, and during summer vacation. Hobby schools develop skills in anything from playing music and sports to making model planes. Families pay around one-tenth of the cost, and the government pays the rest.

This is an Estonian gymnasium. Different gymnasiums specialize in certain subjects, ranging from languages to sciences.

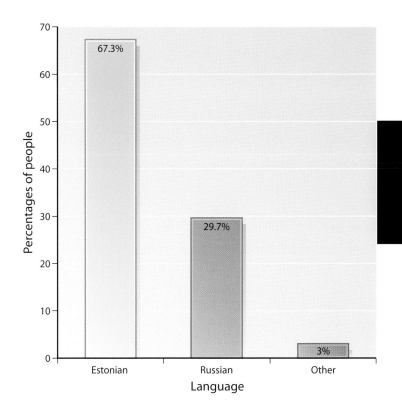

This bar graph shows the languages spoken in Estonia and the percentage of people who speak them.

Estonia has 3 doctors per 1,000 citizens, which is around the same as other European countries.

Health care

Estonia funds free health care—including family doctors, health specialists, and hospitals—from taxes paid by its citizens. However, people pay extra for certain things, such as to stay overnight in a hospital or receive a home visit from a doctor. The health care system and outdoor lifestyles of many Estonians keep the population quite healthy. The World Health Organization (WHO) placed Estonia 77th out of 190 countries in its ranking of world health systems in 2000.

Some common health problems in Estonia are actually caused by the outdoor lifestyle. Encephalitis (inflammation of the brain) can be caught from tick bites. Ticks are small **parasites** that normally live on the blood of deer and other wild mammals. They can get onto people walking through areas of Estonia where these animals live. People swimming in some Estonian rivers and lakes can swallow **bacteria** that gives them diarrhea.

Communication

There is excellent cell phone reception all over Estonia, even on remote islands. Nearly all Estonians use cell phones, but not just to chat and text. They use their cell phones to link to their bank accounts and pay for anything from parking tickets and medical prescriptions, to shopping. The government provides different mobile services. For example, Estonians can vote in government elections from their mobile phones, or receive text reminders that they need a new passport.

YOUNG PEOPLE

In many countries, students must wait weeks for their exam results to be sent to them. In Estonia, students get a text sent to their cell phone with their results as soon as the papers have been graded!

In Estonian cities, people can access the Internet for free almost anywhere, whether they are walking about, at home, in school, or at work.

Culture: Saunas, Singing, and Sports

There are several different **cultures** in Estonia. A *Mulk* is someone who comes from Mulgimaa (Mulkland) in south Estonia and speaks the area's language, *Mulgi*. President Ilves is a *Mulk* and often wears the traditional *Mulgi* black robes.

The Old Believers are a group of Russian Orthodox **Christians** who live apart from most Estonians. They use candles instead of electricity, and ban coffee and smoking.

The Seto people traditionally wear embroidered clothing. They have their own ruler and worship their **ancestors**, sometimes by leaving food on their graves. Most people in Estonia are not religious, but they enjoy traditional Christian festivals, such as Christmas.

Married Seto women wear *suur solg*, which are silver breast plates decorated with coins. They inherit these from their mothers.

National culture

Most Estonians value their natural landscape, and an important part of their culture is enjoying the outdoors. They pick berries and wild mushrooms and make jams and pickles from their wild produce. Many Estonians enjoy camping in the woods when they can. Taking a sauna is a very common weekend ritual. There are private and public saunas throughout the country, where people sit with few or no clothes on in hot steam rooms to relax.

Once they are hot, after a sauna in a hut like this one, Estonians may cool down by rolling in the snow.

Daily life

Top tips for a trip to the sauna:

- Sit on a towel—even wooden benches get hot in the sauna.
- Hot air rises, so the higher you sit inside the sauna, the hotter it will be.
- Saunas usually have very hot stones heated by fires. Don't pour water on the stones, or it will get even steamier.
- Don't be surprised if locals hit themselves with birch branches—they do this to increase their circulation.
- After 10 minutes or less, cool down with a cold shower. Estonians often jump into the nearest lake!

Music

Folk music is very important to Estonians. It is part of the country's history and legends, and also reminds people of the struggle for independence. The biggest musical gatherings in Estonia happen every five years at the National Song and Dance festival. Hundreds of thousands of Estonians come to hear choirs of up to 20,000 sing. They sing folk songs as well as works by Estonian classical composers, such as Arvo Part and Veljo Tormis.

This is a song festival in Tallinn.

Young Estonians listen to rock, heavy metal, hip-hop, jazz, and many other styles of music on their MP3 players. Music produced both in their own country and elsewhere is popular.

YOUNG PEOPLE

Metsatöll is an old Estonian word that means wolf. Today *Metsatöll* is also the name of one of the most popular Estonian bands among young people. Their sound is a mixture of folk—including male choirs, flutes, bagpipes, and mouth harps—and heavy metal, including rock drums, electric guitars, and screaming!

Students in traditional dress are taking part in a song festival in the city of Tartu.

Arts

Most Estonian towns have their own theater and museum. Some have an opera house, outdoor sculptures, and also often hold literary and other arts festivals. Public poetry readings are popular, either of works by past poets or by current stars, such as Jürgen Rooste and Kristiina Ehin. Traditional crafts include wood carving, pottery and glass making, patterned knitwear, and leather craft.

KRISTIINA EHIN (1977–)

Ehin started to write poetry while she was a student at Tartu University, where she studied Estonian folk poems and songs. She writes about themes common in folklore, such as nationality, birthrights, and modern Estonia. One of her poems is called "My Child Was Born With a Cell Phone in its Hand!"

Sports and other activities

The most popular sports in Estonia are basketball, athletics, and soccer. In summer, many people leave the heat of the cities and head for the beach to swim or go boating. They sail boats along the coastline and around the islands of Saaremaa and Hiiumaa, and canoe on the rivers. They also go fishing, walking, and cycling. In winter, many Estonians go cross-country skiing, skating, or ice boating. Ice boats are fitted with skis or runners, like those you get on ice skates, so the boats can slide over ice instead of through water!

KRISTINA ŠMIGUN-VÄHI (1977-)

Kristina is probably the most famous female sports star in Estonia. She has won three Olympic medals for cross-country skiing—two gold medals in 2006 and a silver medal in 2010. She has also won many more medals at other northern European ski championships. Her parents were professional skiers, too.

In 2006, Kristina Šmigun-Vähi became the first Estonian woman to win an Olympic gold medal.

Estonian food

Many Estonians eat a light breakfast of coffee and rye bread with ham, eggs, or cheese. Most have a main meal of cabbage or potato stew with smoked fish or meat at lunchtime. Then they eat a light supper in the evening, such as beetroot salad. They also like berry jams, pickles, and salt herring.

At Christmas, Estonians eat roast pork or goose, sausage, sauerkraut (a type of pickled cabbage), potatoes, and gingerbread cookies. Some of the more unusual Estonian specialities include pig-feet jelly and a soft drink made with rye bread!

Rosolje or beet salad

Ask an adult to help you make this delicious salad.

Ingredients:

Salad
- 8 potatoes
- 4 beets
- 3 eggs
- 3 small pickles
- ½ an onion
- 1–2 pickled herrings (if you like them)

Dressing:
- 1 ½ cups crème fraîche
- 1 tablespoon of mustard
- 2 ½ tablespoons of balsamic vinegar
- ½ teaspoon of brown sugar
- salt and pepper to taste

What to do:

1. Boil the potatoes, beets, and eggs in separate pans.
2. When cool, peel and chop everything into pieces and put into a large bowl.
3. Finely chop the gherkins. Add the pickles, onion, and the pickled herrings to the bowl.
4. Make the dressing by whisking together the crème fraîche, mustard, balsamic vinegar, and brown sugar.
5. Season with salt and black pepper—and enjoy!

Estonia Today

Modern Estonia is very different from the way it was during the many **occupations** of the past. It has developed into a successful, independent European country. In 2011, Tallinn became a European Capital of **Culture**. This is a place identified by the **EU** as having a rich, vibrant local culture. It was a good opportunity for tourists to visit Tallinn and experience its beautiful locations and interesting activities for themselves. It also helped to make the country better known around the world, and to showcase Estonian **innovation**. Modern Estonia is a world leader in the use of cell phone and electronic information technology. In fact, it is sometimes called E-stonia!

Future development

Like any country, Estonia's development depends on many things. For example, the small population will need to manage its **natural resources** carefully to make sure they last. They will also need to make sure that natural **habitats** are protected as much as possible.

Estonia hopes to develop trade and tourism by improving its railroads. It is helping to pay for the Rail Baltica international railroad route planned for completion by 2020. The railroad will connect Finland to Estonia through a long tunnel. To the south, it will connect Estonia to the other Baltic states, Poland, and Germany. Rail Baltica should cut road use in the region, especially by polluting trucks, to help slow **global warming**.

This modern passenger train is leaving from the Balti-Jaam train station in Tallinn.

Estonia has many beautiful sites for visitors to see. This is a view of the domes of the Alexander Nevsky Cathedral in Tallinn.

Fact File

Official name:	Republic of Estonia
Official language:	Estonian
Capital city:	Tallinn
Type of government:	parliamentary republic
Independence date:	August 20, 1991
Bordering countries:	Latvia, Russia
Population:	1,291,170
Largest cities (populations):	Tallinn (386,100)
	Tartu (100,500)
	Narva (66, 980)
Birth rate:	10.37 births per 1,000 people
Life expectancy (total):	72.82 years
Life expectancy (men):	67.45 years
Life expectancy (women):	78.53 years
Ethnic groups (percentage):	Estonian (67.9%)
	Russian (25.6%)
	Ukrainian (2.1%)
	Belarusian (1.3%)
	Finn (0.9%)
	other (2.2%)
Religion (percentage):	**Lutheran** (13.6%)
	Orthodox (12.8%)
	other **Christian** (1.4%)
	(72.2% of Estonians have no religion or regular worship)
Internet users:	969,700
Military service:	469,666 (ages 16–49)
Currency:	**euro** (replaced the *kroon* in 2011)

Main imports: machinery and equipment (35%)
textiles (19%)
mineral fuels (19%)
chemical products (9%)
foodstuff (6%)

Main exports: machinery and equipment (29%)
wood and paper (13%)
metals (10%)
food products (8%)
textiles (5%)
chemical products (less than 5%)

Units of measurement: metric

Natural resources: oil (from shale), timber, phosphorus, limestone, blue clay

Area (total): 17,462 square miles (45,228 square kilometers)—132nd biggest country in the world

Highest point: Great Egg Hill—1,043 feet (318 meters)

Lowest point: Baltic Sea—0 feet/meters

Biggest lake: Lake Peipus—1,373 square miles (3,555 sq km)—5th largest lake in Europe

National animal: the barn swallow

National flower: cornflower

Famous Estonians

Arvo Pärt (classical composer)
Juri Arrak (artist/cartoonist)
Carmen Kass (supermodel)
Kristina Ehin (poet)
Kristina Šmigun-Vähi (cross-country skier)
Lennart Meri (writer, historian, and first president)
Paul Keres (chess player)
Friedrich Kreutzwald (writer of Estonian folklore)
Ruja (rock band)

Life expectancy in Estonia compared with other countries	
Macau	84
Japan	82
Italy	80
UK	79
USA	78
Morocco	75
Estonia	73
Iraq	70
Russia	66
Ethiopia	55
Angola	38

Estonians can expect to live much longer than Angolans, but not as long as people in Macau or Japan.

Estonia's national anthem

In times of Russian and Soviet **occupation**, the national anthem was banned in Estonia. However, Estonians listening to Finnish radio could hear their anthem's tune, because it is the same one used in Finland's national anthem!

My native land, my joy—delight,
How fair thou art—how bright!
For nowhere in the world around
Can ever such a place be found
So well belov'd, from sense profound,
My native country dear!

My tiny crib stood on thy soil,
Whose blessings eased my every toil.
With my last breath my thanks to thee,
For true to death I'll ever be,
O worthy, most belov'd and fine,
My dearest country mine!

May God in Heaven thee defend,
My own, my dearest land!
May He be guard, may He be shield,
For ever bless and guardian wield
Protection for all deeds of thine,
My own, my dearest land!

How to say...

In the Estonian language, descriptions of weather are often based on ancient beliefs about "powers" controlling natural processes:

külma käes in the hand of the cold (cold weather)
külma vihma in the hand of rain (wet weather)
külma päikese in the hand of sun (sunny weather)

Timeline

BCE is short for before the Common Era. BCE is added after a date and means that the date occurred before the birth of Jesus Christ, for example, 450 BCE.

CE is short for Common Era. CE is added after a date and means that the date occurred after the birth of Jesus Christ, for example, 720 CE.

around 5000 BCE	Northern Asian **tribes** settle in the Baltic area. They are believed to be the **ancestors** of the Estonian **ethnic group**.
800 BCE	Vikings and other Scandinavian forces conquer parts of Estonia
1230 CE	Teutonic Knights invade Estonia and establish the city of Reval, later called Tallinn
1346	Estonia and the entire Baltic region is ruled by German forces
1558–1583	The Livonian War ends German rule. Estonia is split among Polish, Lithuanian, and Swedish control.
1629	Sweden rules the whole of Estonia
1632	First Estonian university at Tartu
1700–1721	Russian troops invade during the Great Northern War
1739–1816	Estonian peasants lose their possessions and power to Russian and remaining German landowners
1869	The first nationwide song festival in Tartu takes place
1914–1918	During World War I, Russian troops are forced to leave the Baltic area. For a short while, Estonia remains unoccupied.

1918–1920	The Estonian War of Independence leads to Russian withdrawal. Estonia becomes independent.
1940	During World War II (1939–1945) Estonia is forced to become part of the **Soviet Union**
1941	**Nazi** troops invade Estonia
1944	The Soviet army returns
1945–53	80,000 Estonians are sent to Siberian **labor camps**
1989	A chain of people is formed across the Baltic States to protest against the Soviet **occupation**
1991	The Republic of Estonia (Eesti Vabariik) is established in August
2004	Estonia becomes a member of the **EU** and **NATO**
2011	Estonia adopts the **euro** as its **currency**

Glossary

ally country that has agreed to help another country, usually to fight wars against a shared enemy

amphibian type of animal that lives both in water and on land, such as frogs

ancestor member of someone's family, who has been dead for a long time

bacteria smallest types of living things, some of which cause diseases

bog type of wetland with soft, wet ground

Christian related to the religion based on the teachings of Christ, or a person of that religion

conservation protection of something, especially rare natural environments, from damage or loss

culture practices, traditions, and beliefs of a society

currency banknotes and coins accepted in exchange for goods and services

economy to do with the money, industry, and jobs in a country

ethnic group group of people who identify with each other because of their shared race, culture, or religion

euro type of currency used in many European countries

EU (European Union) organization of European countries with shared political and economic aims

export transport and sell goods to another country

famine serious and widespread shortage of food

global warming increase in temperatures around the world, caused by gases, such as carbon dioxide in the atmosphere

habitat environment where a plant or animal lives

head of state main public representative of a country, such as a queen or president

humid when air is warm or damp

import bring in a product, resource, or service from another country

innovation new idea or way of doing something

labor camp prison where inmates are forced to do hard physical work

Lutheran follower of Christianity with beliefs that are different from those of Catholics

medieval relating to the Middle Ages, a period in European history between 500 CE and the 1400s

mineral solid, nonliving substance that occurs naturally

NATO (North Atlantic Treaty Organization) organization that includes the United States, Canada, and many European countries in which members give each other military help

natural resource supply of a naturally occurring substance, such as oil, that a country can use and sell

Nazi member of the National Socialist Party in Germany in the 1930s and 1940s

occupation when people from one region or country take over another by force

parasite type of living thing that lives on or in another living thing, and gets all their food from it

peat type of soil that forms from rotted plants, sometimes cut and dried out for use as fuel

persecution when people are unfairly or cruelly treated because of their ethnic group, skin color, religion, or political beliefs

plague widespread disease that kills or affects many people

plantation large area planted with one type of tree or crop for harvest and sale

pollution when substances make water, air, or soil dirty and harmful to living things

revolution when large numbers of people try to change the government, using either peaceful or violent protest

service industry part of a country's economy that provides services, such as hotels, shops, and schools, for its people

Soviet Union communist state made up of Russia and its former empire, in existence between 1922 and 1991

tribe independent social group, historically often made up of nomadic peoples

Find Out More

Books

Hiisjarv, Piret, and Ene Hiiepuu. *Looking at Estonia*. Minneapolis, MN: Oliver Press, 2006.

Libal, Autumn. *Estonia* (The European Union). Broomall, PA: Mason Crest, 2005.

Moseley, Christopher. *Colloquial Estonian*. New York: Routledge, 2008.

Spilling, Michael. *Estonia, 2nd edition*. Tarrytown, NY: Marshall Cavendish, 2010.

Websites

www.elfond.ee/en
Visit the Estonian Fund for Nature website to find out more about habitat conservation in Estonia.

www.estonica.org/en
You'll find a lot of information about Estonian history, culture, society, and more on this website.

www.culturepoint.ee
This website provides a glimpse of the range of cultural activities available in Estonia.

www.erm.ee/?lang=ENG&node=509&parent=429
Discover the history of Estonian rye bread! You can also see some pictures of breadmaking at the beginning of the 20th century.

www.estonia.gov.uk/eng/estonia/tallinn_2011
Find out about the Estonian European Capital of Culture celebrations in 2011.

www.estonia.gov.uk/estonia/photo_gallery
Have a look at the amazing pictures of Estonia on this website.

Places to visit

If you ever get the chance to go to Estonia, here are just some of the many places you could visit:

Tallinn old town, Estonia

This is one of the best-preserved medieval towns in Europe. You can take a walking tour to see its cobbled streets and red roofs, as well as some important cultural landmarks, such as the Alexander Nevsky Cathedral.

Estonian Open Air Museum, near Tallinn

Visit this interesting museum to learn more about Estonia's past, its folk tales, and foods. You can also see displays of wooden structures and buildings similar to those found in villages in the 1700s and 1800s, such as windmills, watermills, farm houses, and taverns.

Estonian National Museum, Tartu

This museum is a good place to go to see traditional Estonian costumes and many other aspects of life in the country through the ages.

Kadriorg Palace, Tallinn

This palace was built in the 1700s by the Russian ruler Peter the Great. It was a summer residence for his wife Catherine. The palace is surrounded by beautiful gardens and parks, and there is an art museum in its grounds.

Pärnu

Known as Estonia's "summer capital," this seaside city offers long, sandy beaches and plenty of fun outdoor activities. You can go swimming, roller skating, water skiing, and sailing, or visit the many shops and restaurants in the city.

Topic Tools

You can use these topic tools for your school projects. Trace the map onto a sheet of paper, using the thick black outlines to guide you.

The colors of the stripes in the Estonian flag are symbolic of the country and its people. Blue represents the lakes dominating the country and also loyalty. Black represents the peat-rich soil and the troubled past. The white band represents snow and ice, but also the country's bright future. Copy the flag design and then color in your picture. Make sure you use the right colors!

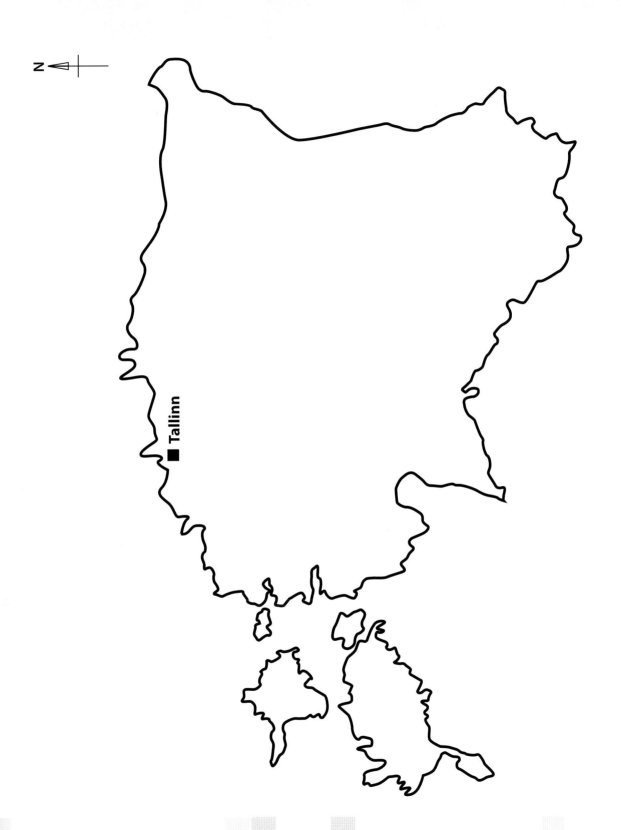

Tallinn

N

Index

Titles in the series